The Lap-Time Song and Play Book

The Lap-Time Song and Play Book

Edited by **JANE YOLEN**

With musical arrangements by **ADAM STEMPLE**

Pictures by **MARGOT TOMES**

HBJ

HARCOURT BRACE JOVANOVICH, PUBLISHERS

San Diego   New York   London

Library of Congress Cataloging-in-Publication Data
The lap-time song and play book.
For piano; with interlinear words.
Summary: A collection of sixteen nursery songs, each with a historic note,
musical arrangement, and instructions for accompanying activities.
Includes such titles as "The Noble Duke of York,"
"I'm a Little Teapot," and "Ride a Cock-Horse."
1. Children's songs. 2. Games with music. [1. Songs.
2. Singing games. 3. Nursery rhymes. 4. Finger play]
I. Yolen, Jane. II. Stemple, Adam. III. Tomes,
Margot, ill.
M1997.L335   1989   88-752289
ISBN 0-15-243588-3

First edition   A B C D E

HBJ

The paintings in this book were done in gouache on Strathmore watercolor paper.
Music and text composition by A-R Editions, Madison, Wisconsin
The display and text type were set in Goudy Old Style.
Color separations were made by Bright Arts, Ltd., Hong Kong.
Printed and bound by Tien Wah Press, Singapore
Typography and book design by Judythe Sieck
Production supervision by Rebecca Miller Garcia and Warren Wallerstein

*To my own mother, Isabelle Yolen, who shared
many of these lap songs with my brother and me*
—J.Y.

For Betsy
—A.S.

For Betty Main
—M.T.

Table of Contents

◆

The Noble Duke of York

This British Mother Goose rhyme refers to Frederick Augustus, Duke of York, who was the second son of England's King George III (1760–1820). The Duke commanded an unsuccessful campaign in Flanders, and the hill described is Mount Cassel in Belgium. However, it is doubtful that either the Duke or his soldiers acted as the verse suggests.

◆

TO PLAY: The child sits on your lap. You salute each other for the opening line. At the words "ten thousand men" the saluting hand waggles its fingers vigorously. Then the grown-up marches his or her second and third fingers up the child's body—over the tummy, up the chest, down the back, then back again—in rhythm with the tune.

Jauntily

Oh, the no-ble Duke of York, He had ten thou-sand men. He marched them up to the top of the hill, And he marched them down a - gain.

2. And when they were up, they were up.
And when they were down, they were down.
And when they were only halfway up,
They were neither up nor down.

(Repeat first verse.)

Hickory Dickory Dock

This popular game song was first published as a limerick in an English children's book called Tom Thumb's Pretty Song Book *in 1744. Some scholars think the "hickory dickory dock" nonsense is related to counting rhymes, such as shepherds in Westmoreland used to count their sheep, where* hevera *meant eight,* devera *meant nine, and* dick *meant ten.*

◆

TO PLAY: Using your first two fingers like a pair of legs, walk up the child's arm. At "the clock struck one," give the child one kiss, as noisy as possible. Then let the fingers run away down the same arm.

These next two are not songs, but simple tuneless finger games.

Here Is the Church

This British ditty is one of the most popular of all finger games and is recited throughout the English-speaking world.

Here is the church,
And here is the steeple,
Open the door
And see all the people.

◆

TO PLAY: Lock the fingers, knuckle to knuckle. *That* is the church. Place pinkies together in an arch. *That* is the steeple. Now open thumbs wide as if opening a door while simultaneously pointing locked fingers upward. On the line "see all the people," waggle the fingers.

Here Are My Lady's Knives and Forks

Less popular, this English rhyme is played in a very similar way.

Here are my lady's knives and forks,
Here is my lady's table.
Here is my lady's looking glass,
And here is the baby's cradle.

◆

TO PLAY: Lock the fingers, knuckle to knuckle, then invert so that the fingers are pointing upward. *Those* are the knives and forks. Invert so that the knuckles are upward. *That* is the table. Face knuckles toward you. *That* is the looking glass. Turn knuckles up again in a rocking motion, and *that* is the cradle.

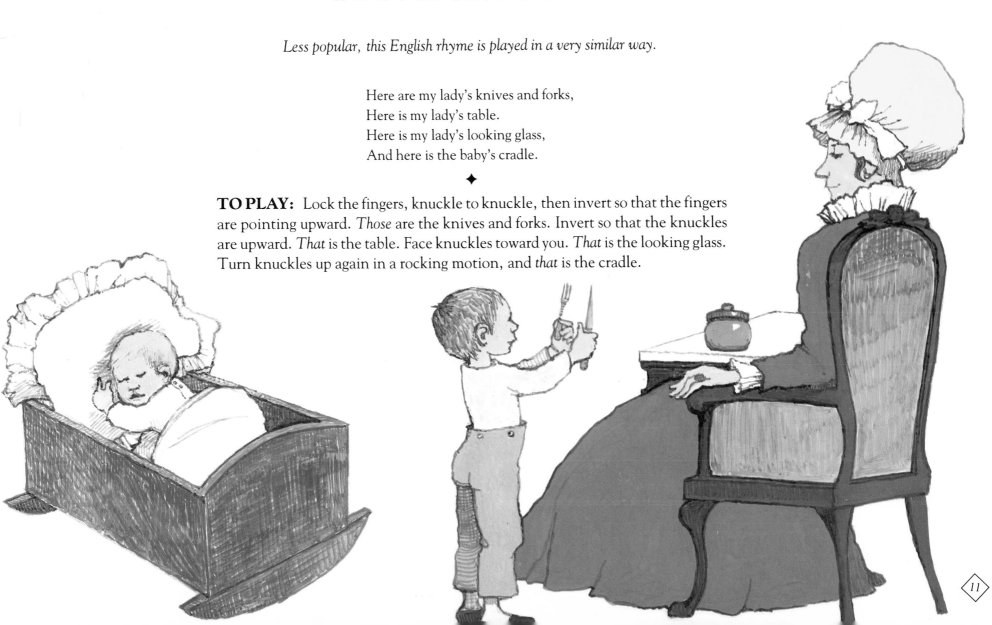

I'm a Little Teapot

This American ditty is very popular in kindergarten classrooms. There is another version, by science-fiction writer Ed Bryant, that goes: "I'm a stegosaurus, short and stout. Here is my tail and here is my snout. When I get real hungry, you can hear me shout. GRRRRRRRRR." And at the growl, the singer raises his or her hands high overhead and leaps upon the closest listener.

◆

TO PLAY: Sit or stand straight for the first line. Place left hand on hip for the handle, and extend right arm—bent at wrist and elbow—upward for the spout. Getting "steamed up" means getting excited, so excitement should show in the face. Then at the "tip me over, pour me out" lines, adult and child should bend over at the waist toward the extended arm, as if pouring tea out of the spout. For the second verse, simply follow the words.

here is my spout. When I get all steamed up,

hear me shout: "Just tip me o - ver, pour me out."

2. I'm a special teapot, it is true,
Here, let me show you what I can do.
I can change my handle and my spout.
Just tip me over, pour me out.

The Eensy Weensy Spider

This is an American play-party song that has British roots. It is now a favorite in schools across the country.

◆

TO PLAY: Place your right thumb on left forefinger, left thumb on right forefinger. Then swivel fingers alternately in a walking motion as the spider goes up the spout. Move hands up and down for rain. When the sun comes out, make a circle with thumbs and forefingers and raise it slowly in the rhythm of the song. Then begin walking with fingers again.

The een-sy ween-sy spi-der went up the wa-ter spout.

Patty-Cake, Patty-Cake

This British rhyme celebrates pat-a-cakes, *small cakes with currants still popular in England. Some scholars read a political and religious background into the song, pointing out that Beker's-man was an old Saxon word for the priest and that "mark it with T" meant to make the sign of the cross over the wafer given at communion. Most American mothers and fathers sing "mark it with B" for "baby." The earliest printing of the song was in 1698 as a children's song in Thomas d'Urfey's* The Campaigners.

◆

TO PLAY: The child sits on your lap facing you. Clap hands with child for the first four lines. Then, miming a baker making dough balls, "roll it and prick it," and as if writing on it, mark it with a T or a B or even the child's own initial. For "put it in the oven" turn palms upward and gently poke into the child's tummy, as if putting dough into the oven.

With a gentle bounce

Pat-ty-cake, pat-ty-cake, ba-ker's man, Bake me a cake _ as fast as you can.

Roll it and prick it and mark it with B, Put it in the o-ven for ba-by and me.

Where Is Thumbkin?

This American ditty is a simplification of the English finger-dance "Dance, Thumbkin, Dance," in which each of the fingers is given a name: Thumbkin, Foreman, Longman, Ringman, and Littleman. In fact, at one time every finger had a name in the English language, depending upon the area in which one lived, not just the thumb and pinkie. Thumbs have been known as "Tom Thumbkin," "Tommy Tomkins," "Bill Milker," "Thumbiekins," and "Thumpkins," among others.

◆

TO PLAY: On the questions "Where is Thumbkin?", first one thumb and then the other is brought up. At the lines "Here I am," the thumbs bob one after the other. On the conversational "How are you today, sir?" and its answer, the thumbs each describe a circle, as if speaking to each other. On the "Run and hide" lines, first one, then the other hand disappears behind the singer's back. The same is done for each successive finger.

2. Where is point finger? . . . etc.

3. Where is long finger? . . . etc.

4. Where is ring finger? . . . etc.

5. Where is pinkie? . . . etc.

These next two are not songs, but simple tuneless games.

Brow Bender, Eye Peeper

This English feature-counting game has many variations. The first four lines were printed in Tommy Thumb's Song Book *in 1788. The popular camp song "Hands on Myself" is a modern version of this game.*

Brow Bender,
Eye Peeper,
Nose Dropper,
Mouth Eater,
Chin Chopper,
Knock at the door,
Ring the bell,
Lift up the latch,
Walk in,
Take a chair,
Sit by there,
And how do you do this morning?

TO PLAY: The child sits facing you on your lap or in a highchair. You touch the child's features one at a time: brow bender—forehead; eye peeper—eyes; nose dropper—nose; mouth eater—mouth; chin chopper—chin. At "Knock at the door," you tickle the child's chin. "Ring the bell" is for lightly pulling the ear. At "Lift up the latch" you raise the child's nose lightly and then pop your forefinger into his or her mouth.

This Little Piggie

Called by folk rhyme collectors Iona and Peter Opie "the best known toe- or finger-counting rhyme in the English language," the piggie verse has many variants. The cry of the little piggies is sometimes "week week," sometimes "wee wee wee," and is always followed by a child's laughter.

This little piggie went to market.
This little piggie stayed home.
This little piggie had roast beef.
This little piggie had none.
And this little piggie cried, "Wee! Wee! Wee!"
All the way home.

◆

TO PLAY: This is most successful as a toe-counting rhyme, the first little piggie being the child's big toe, which you hold on to gently between your thumb and forefinger while reciting the line. Then on to the next, and the next, and the next. When you come to "Wee! Wee! Wee!" let go of the toe and tickle the child until he or she roars with laughter.

John Brown's Baby

Sung to the tune of the "Battle Hymn of the Republic," this silly play-party game is a pantomime that gets more and more elaborate with each repetition.

◆

TO PLAY: With the child sitting next to you (not on your lap), sing the song through once with no miming. On the second time through, the word "baby" is left out and the rhythm space is taken up with a pantomime of a baby being rocked in the arms. On the next run-through, the baby substitute continues and, in addition, the word "cold" is dropped, and either a sneeze or a cough takes its rhythmical place. The next time through, in addition to these substitutions, the word "chest" is dropped, and the pantomime is a fist against the chest. The next time, "rubbed it" is replaced by a circular rubbing motion on the chest. The last time, "camphorated" is dropped, and the substitute is nose-holding, meaning a terrible smell.

Ride a Cock-Horse

This rhyme has been traced back to the 1600s and may have referred to Queen Elizabeth I, Lady Godiva, or a British lady named Celia Fiennes who rode throughout England in 1697. A cock-horse is another name for a child's hobbyhorse or anything a child rides astride, like a parent's knee. In the sixteenth century, however, it also referred to a large or high horse or stallion. In some versions the white horse is black, the fine lady an old lady, and Banbury Cross, Coventry Cross.

◆

TO PLAY: The child sits astride your knee and is bounced up and down rhythmically on the first two lines. When the rings on her fingers are mentioned, take the child's hands one at a time and kiss them. Then make kisses in the direction of each of the feet for the bells on her toes. Return to the bouncing for the final line.

Ride a cock-horse to Ban-bur-y Cross, To see a fine la-dy up - on a white horse.

Rings on her fing-ers and bells on her toes, And she shall have mus-ic where ev - er she goes.

This Is the Way the Farmer Rides

This song is closely related to an old nursery rhyme, "This Is the Way the Ladies Ride," which is the English version of this American lap game.

◆

TO PLAY: The child sits on your legs facing you (or in some versions, the child sits on your crossed legs). To the rhythm of the song the child is bounced heartily (farmer), daintily (ladies), jauntily (gentlemen), and then wildly (with the child's own name), the final time ending with the child slipping down between your legs. Always remember to keep firm hold of the child's hands the whole time!

With a rolling motion

This is the way the farm-er rides, The farm-er rides, the farm-er rides.

This is the way the farm-er rides, So ear-ly in the morn-ing.

2. This is the way the ladies ride,
   The ladies ride, the ladies ride.
   This is the way the ladies ride,
   So early in the morning.

3. This is the way the gentlemen ride, etc.

4. This is the way that (baby) rides, etc.

These next two are not songs, but simple tuneless games.

Trot, Trot to Boston

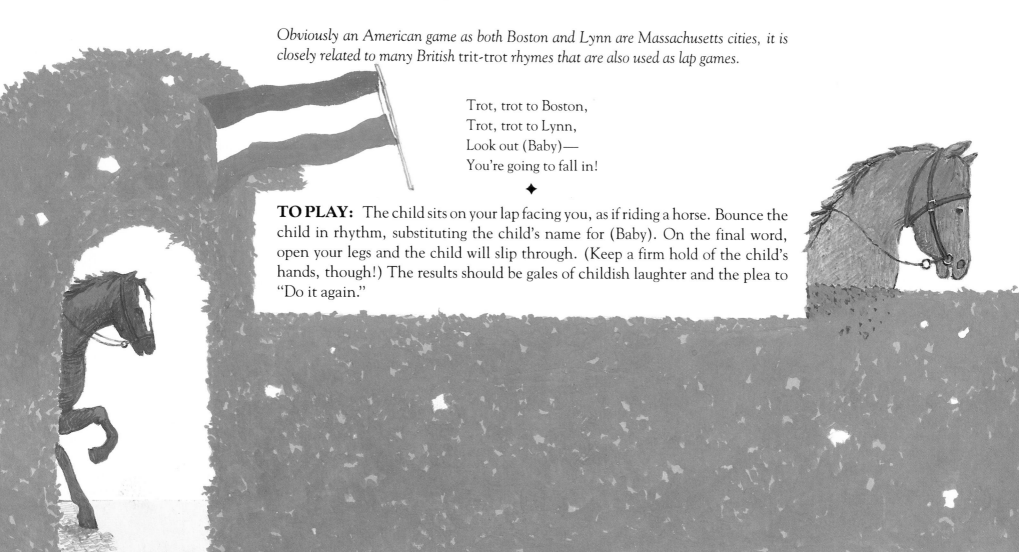

Obviously an American game as both Boston and Lynn are Massachusetts cities, it is closely related to many British trit-trot rhymes that are also used as lap games.

Trot, trot to Boston,
Trot, trot to Lynn,
Look out (Baby)—
You're going to fall in!

◆

TO PLAY: The child sits on your lap facing you, as if riding a horse. Bounce the child in rhythm, substituting the child's name for (Baby). On the final word, open your legs and the child will slip through. (Keep a firm hold of the child's hands, though!) The results should be gales of childish laughter and the plea to "Do it again."

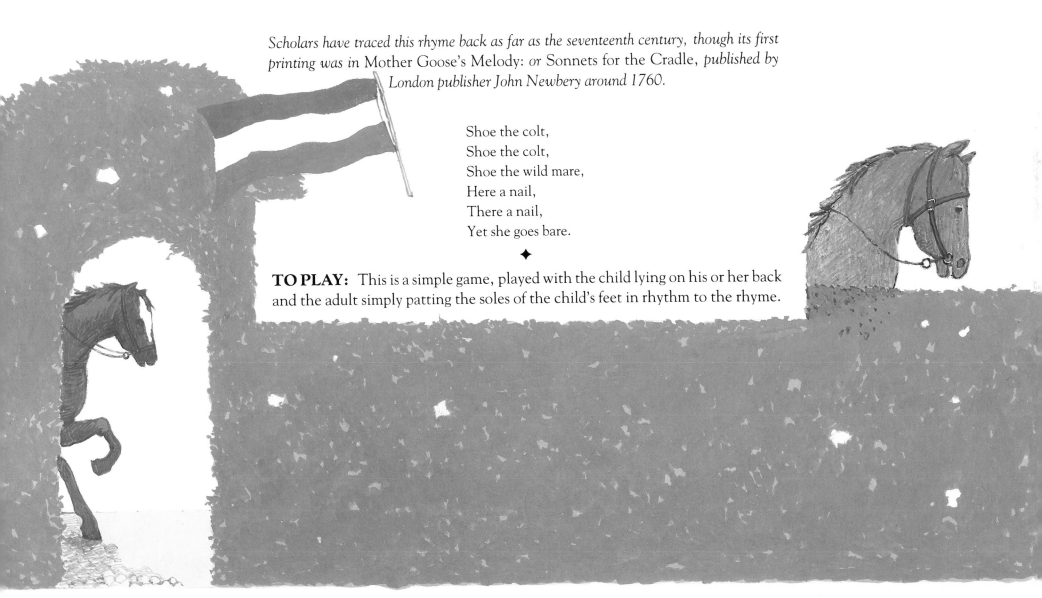

Shoe the Colt

Scholars have traced this rhyme back as far as the seventeenth century, though its first printing was in Mother Goose's Melody: or Sonnets for the Cradle, *published by London publisher John Newbery around 1760.*

Shoe the colt,
Shoe the colt,
Shoe the wild mare,
Here a nail,
There a nail,
Yet she goes bare.

◆

TO PLAY: This is a simple game, played with the child lying on his or her back and the adult simply patting the soles of the child's feet in rhythm to the rhyme.

Down by the Station

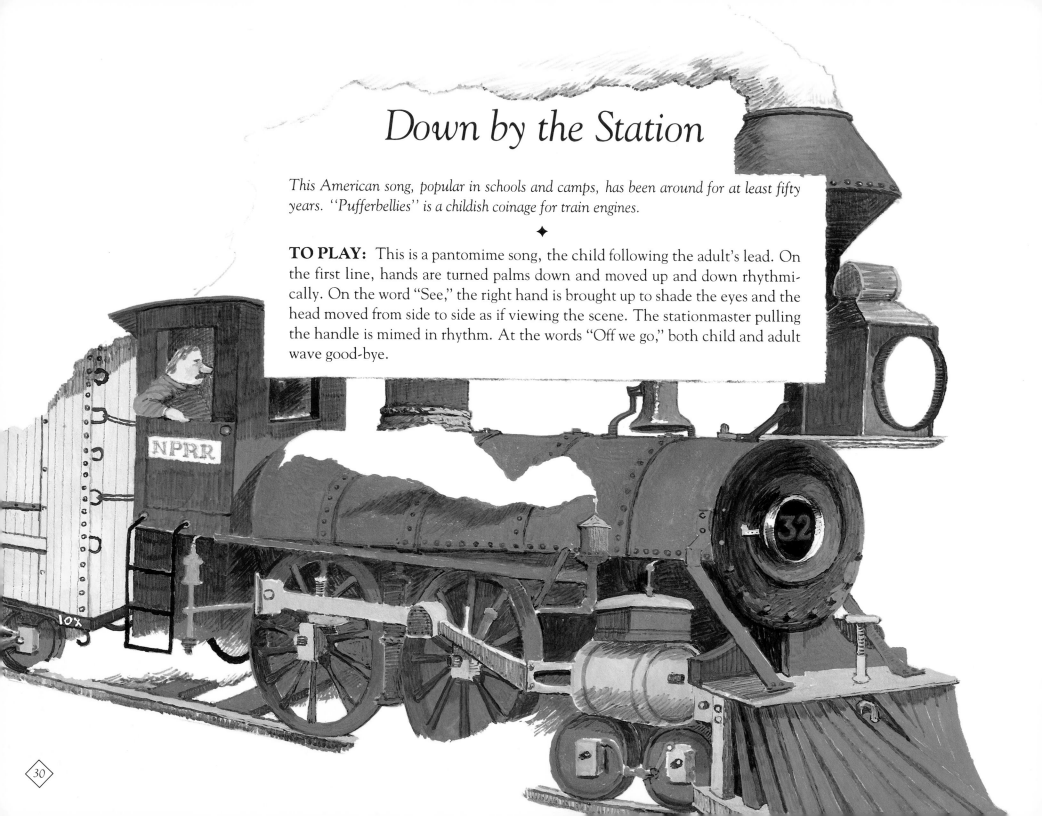

This American song, popular in schools and camps, has been around for at least fifty years. "Pufferbellies" is a childish coinage for train engines.

◆

TO PLAY: This is a pantomime song, the child following the adult's lead. On the first line, hands are turned palms down and moved up and down rhythmically. On the word "See," the right hand is brought up to shade the eyes and the head moved from side to side as if viewing the scene. The stationmaster pulling the handle is mimed in rhythm. At the words "Off we go," both child and adult wave good-bye.

About Lap Songs

Every nation has its own lullabies and lap songs; the first to soothe the babies to sleep, and the second to play with them when they are awake and wanting attention. These songs and games have come down to us over the centuries—mother to daughter, father to son, mouth to ear, with all the laughter in between.

Lap songs are not just entertainments, though. Words are connected to actions, sounds to rhythms; parts of the body are pointed at and named. Lap songs, then, can be a parent's first attempts at teaching; but it is a gentle, playful schooling. What is being taught is much more than mere words, actions, and rhythms. Love is the matter between parent and child.

Most of the songs and games in this book are ones I played with my three children when they were small. My daughter's favorite was "Trot, Trot to Boston," and she would have had me play it endlessly if my legs had not given out after the first eight or nine times. My sons were great fans of "This Is the Way the Farmer Rides" and "This Little Piggie." I expect they will pass these same songs and games on to their own children when they have them, hauling the words back from recesses of memory where they have been stored since childhood. In case you have forgotten some or do not know certain of these lap games, I have put them here, a present from our family to yours.

—Jane Yolen